Speak Life Series:

Bedroom Secrets

Second Edition

by
Deborah Leaner

Y-Not Publishing
Mitchellville, Maryland

If you would like more information about Deborah Leaner Ministries, please visit us on the web at: www.deborahleaner.com

Edited by:
Laura Jackson
Marilyn Hardy

Book design by:
Patricia A. Jackson

ISBN: 978-0-9816888-2-4
Make Your Mouth A Ministry Speak Life Series
Bedroom Secrets Second Edition
Printed in the United State of America

Table of Contents

Author's Preface

Why this book, and what is its purpose? You can probably find the answer in every whisper I hear from women all over the United States.

I noted some years ago a growing number of women devastated by the onset of infidelity in their marriages and the expectation to just forgive and forget. The reaction to this expectation has caused some women to feel lifeless, lonely, lost and worthless. For this kind of woman, simply forgiving and forgetting would be the same as catching her man in the very act of infidelity.

I've never seen anything that has damaged marriages so deeply. The wreckage appears in the form of broken homes, angry children and stiff-necked communities. This book offers some "Speak Life Moments" aimed at the multitude of marriages that are being attacked by attitudes of confusion, brokenness and bitterness that seek to steal, kill and destroy.

This book, I trust, will serve in some small way to bring attention to the need to Speak Life into our marriages and relationships before major problems occur. In this material, I speak frankly and openly to women about real issues affecting our marriages and sexuality. The goal isn't to offend; rather, "Dear Bedroom Secrets" truthfully discusses subjects that we've avoided for far too long due to shame, fear, embarrassment or lack of knowledge. Speaking Life can heal the brokenhearted and create a pathway to forgiveness.

Note: The responses in Chapters 1, 2, 3 and 5 provide "SisterGirl" with five important points to reflect on in answer to her inquiries. And, in Chapter 4 we omit the five points and respond directly to each apprehension made by the inquirer.

Finally, at the end of each Chapter, space has been allocated for your own notes to be written as God speaks to you.

Deborah Leaner

My Love is Mine
and I am His

Song of Solomon 2:16

Dear Reader:

How nice it is to be with you once again! It's a privilege to share my heart with you as I reveal some Speak Life Moments. Thank you for meeting here. Take a seat in a relaxing place and have a cup of tea. Retreat into a place where secrets can flow through your senses and soul.

I believe you'll find this conversation intimate, refreshing, romantic and transforming.

Ah, it's also my desire that forgiveness will release any of your inhibitions so love can flow freely in your life.

Chapter One
The Love Altar

One of the hardest storms for a marriage to weather is infidelity. Cheating shakes the foundation of the marriage and changes the way the couple relates to each other for life. Inevitably, if a man cheats it's generally more acceptable than if a woman cheats. If the woman cheats, she might be scorned, maligned or ridiculed. In some societies, she could even be stoned.

Things are changing, and so is the number of women cheating on their husbands in the 21st century. When women whisper in my ear, they aren't always crying about their husbands' unfaithfulness. Instead, they're often confessing their own infidelities. When I listen to these stories, it's clear to me that she needed more emotional intimacy and he needed more sex and respect. I hear it over and over again. We need healing (sexual and emotional) to restore our marriages properly. We need to create a love altar.

Dear Bedroom Secrets:

My marriage is such a disappointment. I'm so lonely. Why haven't things turned out the way I thought they would?

When I was a little girl, I read stories like Cinderella, Snow White, and Sleeping Beauty. All of the stories had the same ending—the handsome man rescued the woman, he solved her problems, and they lived happily ever after.

As a teenager, I remember sitting outside on the back porch planning my wedding -- what my dress would look like, how everyone would look at me with admiration. I was about 16 at the time and I hated living at home. I couldn't wait for my knight in shining armor to come and take me away!

I read romance novels all the time back then. The plot in the romance novels followed the same pattern—the woman meets the man and he brings her chocolates, flowers and diamonds. He takes her on romantic escapades to far-away and enchanted places. They fall in love and live happily ever after!

After reading all these romance novels and watching my favorite romantic movies, I thought my husband would show up and rescue me. But in all these years of marriage, he hasn't been willing to stand out in the rain, reciting poetry and telling me how much he loves me and needs me!

In fact, it's just the opposite. I have told my husband over and over that he doesn't make me feel loved. I thought that from the moment we said our wedding vows, we were supposed to live in marital bliss and in "the happily ever after." What a joke!

Let me tell you what happened last night. My husband was watching some stupid football game. (He said he was looking at the playoffs, but who cares?) I decided I'd finally had enough. He wasn't paying me any attention! I interrupted him to share what I felt were my innermost feelings.

I expressed how I had longed to enjoy a more fulfilling marriage with him. I begged him to spend more time with me. I explained to him that I wanted our love relationship to be so deep that we would know each other's thoughts before we even said them aloud. I told him how much I wanted a meaningful, romantic bond with him -- an intertwining of our very souls.

My husband just got up and started heading into another room to finish watching the game. When I yelled at him to give me some kind of response, he just mumbled that I was impossible to please and never satisfied. He headed down into the basement and shut the basement door in my face.

I went to bed alone and cried. Why doesn't my husband

love me? Should I look for another man who will give me the love I truly desire?

Dear SisterGirl,

The answer is never in another man. You need to create a Love Altar.

What is a Love Altar? I'm glad you asked.

A love altar ushers you into a place of intimacy and sharing. This is your place to meet with God and be transparent, open, real and honest without guilt or condemnation.

When you begin to strengthen your relationship with God at the love altar, you'll find answers for your individual and private concerns.

Five Ways to Create Your Love Altar

- **Find a quiet place with little or no distractions**

Mark 1:35 - "Now in the morning, having risen a long while before daylight, He went out and departed to a solitary (deserted) place, and there He prayed.

The discipline of stillness is a faithful response to God's command of *Psalm 46:10—"Be still, and know that I am God."* To be still is to withdraw for a season from your normal activities—work, play, conversation—so you can place yourself, alone and silent, in God's presence. As you wait "there" gaining a distance from the world, God begins to show you things from His perspective. When you let go of work, busyness, and socializing for a time, then you will start to let go as well of ambition, jealousy, unhealthy self-reliance, and a sense of self-importance. You will learn patience and discover tranquility.

- **Make a date with God daily**

Quiet time is a time of meditation whereby you seek a deeper, clearer, fuller understanding of God, yourself, and the world around you. Set aside time to think carefully about what the Lord might be saying to you through Scripture, spiritual reading, or the thoughts He brings to your mind as you reflect.

Your quiet time can be any time of the day or night—God is always available to commune with you—morning, mid-morning, noon, midday, afternoon, early evening, late evening, and night.

Whatever time you set, remember, this is your commitment and your time to be still and abide with the Holy Spirit… *"Abide in Him, and He will abide in you (see John 15:4-5)."*

Draw near to Him with praise, worship, song, prayer, and/or even dance.
Galatians 5:16 – "Walk in the Spirit, and you shall not fulfill the lust of the flesh."

You'll come face-to-face with your weaknesses and limitations during your quiet time with the Holy Spirit. Focusing on your purpose allows you to recognize those weaknesses and limitations in humility and then grow through God's grace despite them.

Two disciplines that can help you find focus is stability and worship. Stability helps you "stay put when you ought to stay put." It's a willingness to work with a situation that God has given you rather than desiring another situation that you might think would be better. It is the refusal to run from a problem.

Worship becomes a discipline when the possibility of joy regarding your situation seems far away. It is a choice of the will (to worship) in spite of what you feel. You'll worship (walk in the Spirit) because God (and your spouse) is *"worthy... to receive glory and honor and power (Revelation 4:11)."* Worship helps you take your eyes off yourself and your problems so that you focus instead on who God is and what He has done for you. When you do, your perspective changes. You find new faith in the Lord and new hope in His future for you (with your spouse).

- **Read His Word**

I Timothy 4:13 -- ... "give attention to reading, to exhortation, to doctrine."

Attend to the reading of God's Word in your public and private life. At the Love Altar, you will remember Scripture that will encourage your heart to be loving, peaceful, and joyful. Fortified by the first three virtues you'll then be able to reach out to your spouse with patience, kindness and goodness, at which point God's grace will guide you to patience, gentleness and self-control. The Holy Spirit, working through you, enables you to have victory over the sinful nature's passions and desires. Your faith must continually lay hold of truth, or you'll be tempted to try to secure victory by self-effort.

- **Meditate on His Word**

Philippians 4:8-- … "whatever things are true, whatever things are noble, whatever things are just, whatever things are pure, whatever things are lovely, whatever things are of good report, if there is any virtue and if there is anything praiseworthy—meditate on these things."

The Word of God instructs you on spiritual disciplines that train you to pay attention to the Holy Spirit. As you prepare to meet with the Holy Spirit during your quiet time—even when your desire dwindles and your "to-do" list shouts—your heart will turn toward Him. As you meditate on His Word, pray, and listen, you'll become more attentive to His voice, and more eager to respond in obedience. Spiritual disciplines help you "walk by the Spirit, and…not carry out the desire of the flesh." They help you watch yourself closely, impressing God's Word on your soul as you keep God in the forefront of your thoughts.

The prosperous life for you involves proper thinking and also includes doing the right thing. As you put what you've learned and received into practice, then you'll enjoy the presence of the God of love and peace in your relationship.

Notes

Notes

Chapter Two
A Matter of the Heart

Long before brokenness occurs in your marriage, subtle cracks begin to form in the foundation of the relationship. Some say that a woman's intuition will notify her of a change in the relationship. These changes could include a spouse working longer hours; distant, more withdrawn behavior; irritability; different phone patterns; changes in sexual behavior; or changes in dress, speech and so on.

Sometimes we see the cracks but we don't act hastily enough to address the problem for fear of creating conflict. At other times, we don't take the warning signs seriously. We tell ourselves that we'll deal with the issue when the children leave home, the baby starts sleeping through the night or some other future time.

Dear Bedroom Secrets:

I am guilty.

When I look back at my failed marriage, I'm filled with regrets. You know that common saying: Hindsight is 20-20. I can see the clues now that led to the breakup, but at the time, I just didn't catch the hints.

I thought we had a pretty typical marriage, I guess. But my husband would grumble that we weren't spontaneous anymore. I would send the kids to grandma on weekends so we could enjoy making love for a couple of hours and have some time together. But I think he felt that was getting routine. I guess he wanted me to drop everything when he came home from work and jump his bones in the front closet while the kids were eating dinner. I don't know -- maybe I should have. But at the time I was up to my eyeballs in kids and homework and the dog and work and life. So I would say hello to him as I rushed about meeting everybody else's needs. He would just kind of quietly come in, sit on the couch and then fall asleep.

I wanted him to help me more. It might have been easier to be wild and sexy if I weren't always washing dishes or wiping noses. I will never forget the day he said, "Why do your hands look like that?" I was so pissed! My hands looked dry and ashy at that moment because I had just finished changing some kid's diaper and washing my hands, that's why! I was always tired and frustrated. I rarely felt appreciated. I felt like I was raising kids by myself while he still had time to be a little boy. He could go play softball and hang out all afternoon. If I wanted to go somewhere, he would ask, "When are you coming back?" Like his own kids were burdens.

Of course, we didn't talk about any of this. I think he resented my life. I didn't have to fight my way through downtown traffic the way he did. I worked in the neighborhood elementary school, so I didn't have a commute. I didn't have the pressure of being the primary breadwinner. But he made more money, got more appreciation from his bosses and peers and worked in his field. Me? I gave up a fulfilling career to type boring letters for the assistant principal. I felt my job was beneath me, but I did it, I thought, for my family. I was close to home and I could be with the children after school. Noble, I guess, but I disappeared in the process, and my husband lost all interest in me.

I remember a strange comment he made about six months before he got involved with a co-worker on his job. We had guests over for a party, and everybody was joking and laughing. I don't remember what caused him to make this statement, but I heard him say to someone, "She loves the dog more than me." That wasn't true, and I thought it was a really strange remark at the time. But I forgot to mention it to him. You know, it got lost in the midst of everything else. I didn't really catch the significance until much later, when he told me he was in love with somebody else.

What if we had just talked about our feelings? What if I just threw a screaming fit and shouted how much I hated my life and my job? What if he got to say how much he felt abandoned and overlooked and out of touch? What would have happened? I wish I could go back to that one conversation. Our divorce was stupid, senseless. Everybody got hurt in the process. If I knew then what I know now, I would do things differently.

My Dear SisterGirl,

It appears that you went to "sleep" during your marriage and therefore weren't responsive to the flashing lights in your relationship. Should you get another opportunity to witness for Christ in your marriage, look for the flashing lights. When the red light is flashing, you should take it as seriously as if a snake crawled right through your house or a fire broke out in your kitchen.

SHUT EVERYTHING DOWN AND RESPOND IMMEDIATELY FROM THE HEART. Send the children away, get rid of any other distractions and begin to speak and listen from the heart. This conversation with your mate should go a little deeper than, "Is something bothering you today?" You must find out what's creating the cracks in your marriage. Give your spouse the opportunity to speak from his heart without retaliation. You should receive the same respect.

According to Scripture, the heart is the center, not only of spiritual activity, but also of all the operations of human life. The heart determines whether a person is wise, pure, upright and good, or vice versa.

Your letter indicates to me that there is some evidence of a "hardness" of heart in that you were inattentive and unconcerned about your spouse's request for spontaneity; presumptuous about how things were going in your marriage; and perhaps a bit rude in some of your responses to him. And, by the way, ask for help if you ever find yourself in this situation again.
Sure, there is regret now. It appears that you "slept" so long that someone else was eager to accommodate and answer his needs. Ecclesiastes 8:11 [paraphrased] say, "When the judgment for a fault is not quickly conceded, the hearts of people are filled with schemes to do wrong." Silence from both of you opened the door for the devourer to enter and destroy that which was deemed divine.

Should an opportunity come up again, use these five helpful ideas to reconnect at the heart level:

Five ways to the Heart of the Matter

- **Develop a mentor relationship with an older, married couple you both respect.**

In Scripture, there is no instance that married men and women mentored couples, per se. However, men and women are given sage directives to mentor younger men and women, respectively, to live in response to God's grace.

Proverbs 5:1-23 advises men to forsake lust (guard against the adulteress or an immoral woman); Proverbs

10:1—15:33 contrast righteous and wicked lives of men and women; and Proverbs 31 is motherly advice to her son about immorality and finding a capable wife. The Book of Ecclesiastes wants men and women to know that life is the gift of God, wise people live life in obedience to God (that includes the decision to be married). Matthew (5:23-37; 43-48) gives precepts of Kingdom life and Titus 2 provides a source of mature guidance to younger men and women (usually in ministry, but is a response to God's grace for everyone).

- **Spend time laughing together**

Most people enjoy being with someone who makes them laugh. Try making fun of yourself; don't be afraid of looking foolish. Humor shows how confident you are and serves as a great icebreaker for married couples. Telling funny stories is a good way to spend time together. For example:

My father told me a story about a neighborhood woman who witnessed two men from the neighborhood rob the local store.

The men knew that the woman saw them rob the store, so they thought that they would approach her to see what she would accept in exchange for not reporting them. So, they offered her $500.00 not to tell anyone. She said it was not enough. Then they offered her $1,000.00 to keep her mouth closed about what she saw. She said it was not enough. They then made their final offer, half of what they took from the store -- $1500.00. The woman said, no, it is not enough . The men said, "What do you want?" She said, "I just want to TELL IT!"

Sometimes stories can soften the heart in a way that will allow both of you to laugh together again.

- **Recreate settings from happier times**

Revisit the restaurant you went to on your first date. How did you feel when he first kissed you? Recall the hopes and dreams that both of you spoke about when you met. Revisit the plans you talked about after the engagement and remember the heartfelt vows you made to each other at the wedding. Did you forget that your marriage is a matter of the heart? For where your treasure is, there you will find your heart.

If you find that you can't reconnect in a respectful way through these channels, think of other things that you can do to indirectly open up communication with your spouse on another level. Watching a movie together, for example, could spark a conversation that gives you a deeper understanding of how the two of you have begun to drift apart.

Addressing an issue head-on is difficult, but in the long run confrontation is much healthier. Talking and listening at the heart level creates true intimacy and leads to great sex. A man creates a stronger bond with his wife by really hearing what she has to say. A woman can get a better response from her man if she uses a loving approach as she monitors her tone and language.

- **Step out of your comfort zone**

Do something that you wouldn't normally do with your mate. Ask questions about your sex life that you wouldn't normally ask. Love on him! Love has a way of finding your heart; it goes much beyond egos. When you step out of your comfort zone, you might find that spark that ignited the flame in the very beginning.

Create some new ideas for the marriage with expectancy- when that happens you'll begin to see your marriage through new lenses. Note: Take these ideas to your Love Altar so that God can order your steps.

Marriages go through cycles of change just as the seasons change – when the seasons change we change with the seasons – you would think that a man was crazy if he were wearing a wool coat on a 100 degree sunny day. So it is when we try and respond to each other in the same way we did in the spring of our marriage as we do in the winter of our marriage. Stepping out of your comfort zone may put you right in step with your marriage.

- **Put your mate back in a place of honor**

Apologize for taking your mate for granted when needed, show humility and ask for forgiveness when applicable. Learn to honor each other by:

1. Honoring each other's right to an opinion
2. Getting to know each other all over again
3. Appreciating each other

4. Listening intently to each other without interrupting (even if you disagree)
5. Developing a deeper/intimate friendship.

For further information, Google People Talk: Enhancing Your Relationship (Fact Sheet by Charlotte Shop Olsen, PH.D., and Extension Specialist Family Systems)

Notes

Notes

Chapter Three
Your Garden of Eden

Lasting love and deep intimacy don't just happen. You've got to be purposeful to keep a marriage going strong despite children, in-laws, job layoffs and other issues that seek to pull you and your honey apart.

One of the key ways to keep the bond between you and your mate healthy is to create a physical space that allows you to shut out the world and love on each other. Start by creating a romantic atmosphere in your bedroom.

Your bedroom should be your Garden of Eden. Just like your love altar, your bedroom should be quiet, visually attractive, soothing and a place of refuge. Enhance your surroundings with fresh linens, flowers, candles and inviting scents. Reduce the clutter and keep children's toys out of your bedroom. Seriously consider removing the television.

Remember, your personal garden should be a soft place. Keep this environment stress and drama free. Your Garden of Eden should be for sleeping, intimacy and for sex.

In your personal Garden of Eden, spend time talking about how to create an environment that intrigues you both and makes you want to become one. While you're at it, talk about your dreams for your relationship. What pleases you sexually? How can you make your sexual relationship even better? Teach your spouse how to love you and ask your mate to do the same.

Dear Bedroom Secrets:

I think I'm losing my mind. My marriage, my sanity -- everything is coming apart at the seams. I just don't know what to do anymore.

My husband and I have been trying to have a baby. We've tried everything. We've been to the specialists. We tried in vitro fertilization. We tried relaxation techniques. We tried praying and fasting. My pastor prayed over us on New Year's Eve. I just knew this would be the year! Still no baby. I can't understand why. All these teenage girls out here laying around and getting pregnant. People throwing babies away in trash cans. I've got a home, a job, a marriage. Why can't I have a baby?

The pressure gets to us both. Cysts and fibroids have made fertility difficult, even with surgery. Plus, I'm getting older. Next year I will be 41. I feel like a failure. I'm damaged goods. I see my husband looking at children when we go out. I think he wonders if he'll ever have a child to carry on his legacy. He won't talk much about it, though, because he doesn't want to upset me. Mostly he just looks tired and worried.

Of course, you typically need to make love to get a baby. But you don't much feel like it when you're thinking about the next hormone shot, the cost of the next round of treatments, the next doctor's visit. We'd have to refinance our house to afford another round of IVF. We maxed out the credit cards a long time ago. That's about all we talk about -- our problems. It can make things seem a little mechanical.

I'm mad at myself, my husband and at God. I don't think I'm asking for too much. I would be a great mother!

My Dear SisterGirl,

It sounds as if you could be a terrific mother! But first, let's work on your level of frustration. Let me share with you some ideas that could possibly calm your spirit and redirect your thinking to a more peaceful place.
As Chapter One suggests, on a daily basis have your "quiet time" at the Love Altar (both you and your

husband, together or separately) and communicate with God your heart's desire. Then I suggest you take a look at your "Garden of Eden" – your bedroom. What's in there? Depending on what is there, let me suggest further that you:

- **Create Your Garden of Eden (with both of you in mind)**

The Garden of Eden is described in Genesis chapters two and three as a perfect place—a type of "paradise" that offered both beauty and sustenance. The word "Eden" from Hebrew means "delight."

Your bedroom should be a delight to enter and reside. Here you'll find peace, tranquility and beauty—not clutter from the office, books and newspapers, soda cans and plates from last night's snack. Your laptop and cell phone should be off limits to this room.

Put some effort into creating a "paradise" where flowers and perhaps even a rock/tabletop fountain can usher you into a serene and tranquil garden-effect, right in your bedroom. The décor in your bedroom will enable you to express the intimacy that God has created for a husband and wife to engage in sexual activity with abandon. By the way, you also can use this space for rest and sleep, too. Talk with each other about how your "Garden" should look.

- **Be yourself in Your Garden of Eden**

In the biblical Garden, Adam and Eve were given the freedom to walk around naked. They wore no clothes! Genesis 2:25 say, "And they were, both naked, the man and his wife, and were not ashamed." There's no mention of Eve's cellulite on her hips and thighs, nor mention of Adam's enormously large belly—or the gash in his side. Likewise in your Garden, there's no need for shame. You and your spouse have been "beautifully and wonderfully made." Be comfortable in your own skin.

- **Make Your Garden A Hiding Place**

Designed with you in mind, your garden is your safe space for each of you to talk about your fears, insecurities and confidential matters. Don't allow the serpent to enter the garden and distract the two of you from your purpose. Pillow talk is for the two of you only. Don't invite outside noise into this place of tranquility to make you doubt what God has established. Satan, in Genesis 3:1, implied that God wasn't good and fair because Adam and Eve couldn't eat the fruit of one of the trees. When you have a relationship with God, through Jesus Christ, you'll know that the devil is a liar and the truth is not in him. Don't allow negative thoughts to enter your garden. God is faithful to provide all that you can ask or imagine.

- **Take Serious Disagreements to Another Place**

Respect your Garden enough to have intense fellowship (arguing) in another designated space. Violence is never acceptable. Remember, God is still in control of you and your temperament; and your Garden is designated as "holy ground."

Before an intense fellowship begins, determine that reconciliation is the end-goal. Reconcile to your spouse before entering your garden. Be transparent, open, real, honest and free of guilt or condemnation. Agree quickly.

- **Experience the Beauty of your Garden**

Embrace and enjoy the fruit of the Garden created just for you. God has endowed you with imagination and resources to manifest the beauty of creation. You'll need to hold fast to some garden tools to nurture and cultivate the fruit of your garden so that it remains sweet.

Major tools to keep around include the Fruit of the Spirit: love/compassion, joy or steadfast delight, kindness and caring, goodness, faithfulness and dependability, gentleness and self-control.

You also need accountability—being subject to one another in the fear of Christ; servanthood—making Jesus Christ the Lord of your marriage; influence - lead your home with discipline and self-assurance; and discernment - comprehend God's design for your life and speak wisdom, speak life… into each other.

Notes

Notes

Chapter Four
Enhancing Your Garden of Eden with Lingerie

Add to the appeal of your Garden of Eden with intimate apparel. As time goes by within a marriage, you can easily slip into an attitude of wearing worn-out, unattractive sleepwear. Yes, it might be comfortable, but flannel nightgowns or boring pajamas don't enhance the atmosphere you're trying to create in this special place.

This can be an exciting assignment for you and your spouse! Spend time talking about lingerie you both would enjoy.

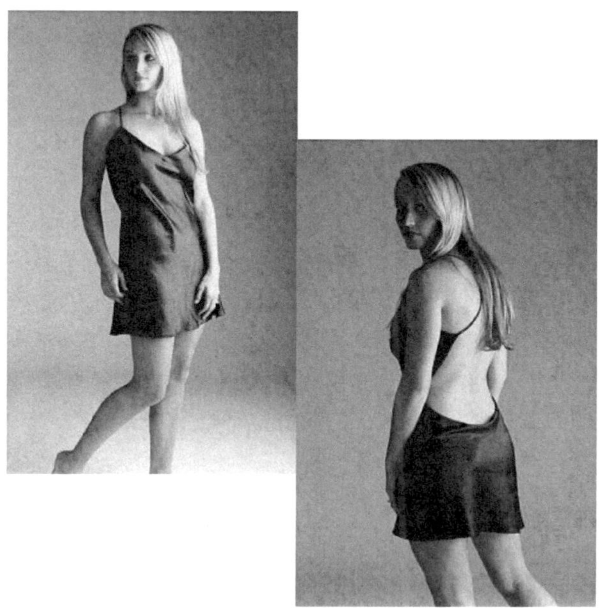

Dear Bedroom Secrets:

My husband and I have reached an impasse in our marriage. If we don't work this out, I think our marriage will come to an end.

My husband has always been rather pushy and obnoxious, especially when he's been drinking. Most of the time I try to go along with what he wants just to keep the peace. Over the years he has tried to push me into more experimental and risqué behavior in the bedroom. When I've resisted in the past, he's always argued me down: "Why not? There's nothing wrong with it. We're two consenting adults." I've gone along with him out of fear that he would just go out there and find someone else. But I feel I have to draw the line somewhere. A man will go as far as you let him, and I worry that my husband will lose all respect for me.

I wasn't raised like this. My mom raised me to be a lady. I'm well respected in my church. I'm close to my first lady. I teach etiquette and charm skills to the debutantes. So when I come home and hear that my husband wants me to swing from the rafters with him or try some new sex toy he saw online -- well, it's difficult for me. How do I line all this up with the word of God? I just don't know if it's OK to watch the dirty movies he wants to watch or do the things he wants to do. I can't find any guidance in my *Bible or from the pulpit.*

This last blow up was the final straw. He had been out drinking, of course, and he came home with some scandalous outfit he saw somewhere. It looked 10 sizes too small, had no crotch in the panties and -- well, let's just say I'm no spring chicken. I'm too old for this foolishness and I told him so, straight out. I don't ask him to parade around in embarrassing, humiliating outfits that show off all his flaws. Why can't he accept me and love me as I am? I have carried his babies and loved him through thick and thin. He wants me to be something I'm not.

We had a big, screaming fight right in the middle of the bedroom just before I was about to get in the bed. All my pent-up resentment came out, and I refused to budge an inch. He says at least he's bringing these things home to me, and other women would love to have some man show that kind of desire. I said if he can find some slut who's willing to put up with his foolishness, he should go right ahead. Then I said he was just looking for something to pump up his old ego so he could pretend he was 20 years younger. Lord, why did I say that? He stomped out of the room and slammed the bedroom door so hard the windows shook. We haven't spoken two words to each other since.

I know I hurt his feelings, but I'm sick of his threats, manipulation and lack of understanding. I'm tired of him seeing me as some raunchy thing to be paraded and exploited -- instead of the wife and treasure I am. I have had enough.

SisterGirl,

I can see that you've waited a long time to sound the alarm for HELP. Let me assure you that your marriage does not have to end. The description that you've given about the relationship with your spouse in this matter, however, reveals that your marriage needs some emergency attention.

Let me also say that it's encouraging to learn that your husband is definitely interested in enjoying his wife in the privacy of your "Garden." So from that perspective I observe that an impending collapse in the marriage is on the horizon. One thing I know for sure: "How you handle conflict is the single most important predictor of whether your marriage will survive."

One of the "flags" that you raise in your letter is the manner in which you were 'raised.' I do recognize that parents influence children's thinking, beliefs and behavior. And in many households, mothers (and maybe fathers, too) don't share intimate details about what to expect in marriage—particularly in regard to sexual behavior. Therefore, women—largely Christian women—have grown up in the "lack of knowledge" and understanding to take pleasure in sex without inhibition. Christian women often look to Scripture to define what is or is not appropriate sexual behavior in marriage.

According to Matthew 19:4-5, when you and your husband married, the commitment between the two of you represents the deepest physical and spiritual union that God has instituted. Genesis 2:24 emphasizes the complete identification of the two personalities of Adam and Eve—the First Couple—in marriage as the complete union of the two.

In regard to theology and psychology, we know that marriage means that the couple must separate emotionally from childhood so as to invest fully in the marriage, and at the same time redefine the lines of connection with families of origin. Simply stated, you and your husband must touch and agree on how to express yourselves sexually. It is wise to build togetherness based on mutual identification, shared intimacy and expanded conscience, both of you, while at the same time setting boundaries to protect each other's autonomy. You can establish a rich and pleasurable sexual relationship and protect it from the invading outside "noise."

As for your husband's "pushy and obnoxious" behavior, it may be impolite, but not unforgivable. Depending on what's driving him to approach you while under the influence of alcohol, it may be just a matter of the two of you having a 'different' conversation in a 'different' designated location (than the bedroom) or it could require more serious attention from a professional source, i.e., marriage and or alcohol dependency counseling.

Additionally, when you have come to grips with how you'll face your own underlying issues (self-perception), then you can look forward to the opportunity to confront your husband's manner of addressing you. For example, if he feels the need to "fuel up" in order to approach you with his requests, then the two of you must confront and master this (and any other) crisis and maintain the strength of the marriage bond in the face of adversity. Create a safe haven within your marriage for difference, anger and conflict.

Let's talk about your "standing" in the society as coach to the debutantes and your friendship with the First Lady of your church. Those roles are great in their respective places. However, you're also the wife of Mr. X, who respects you as such and depends on you to be as skillful in the wife role as the First Lady and the debutantes do in their places.

As wife to Mr. X, when you're home and the magical time to share the fruit of the "garden" is imminent, you'll need to transition from the "church lady/ society/corporate" persona into the vixen your husband desires. Let's face it, as men and women mature (get older), their sexual attentions also mature or get stale, or the sensitivity in certain areas diminishes. Each might need some other stimuli available to enhance sexual pleasure. And, believe me, there are plenty of apparatuses available—some may seem risqué to you because you were not 'raised' that way, but they're nonetheless appealing, especially when sexual attractiveness or sensitivity has become dull or uninteresting for either husband and/or wife.

The Apostle Paul, who, by the way, was not an advocate for marriage unless it was to keep a person from sinning, wrote to the Church people at Corinth his judgment about marriage and Christian service. He encouraged unmarried women to devote their life to the cares of the

Lord. And at I Corinthians 7:33-34 he gives his thoughts to husband and wife. Notice what is said at the end of verse 34(b), "But she who is married cares about the things of the world—how she may please her husband."

Now, I don't know if Paul knew anything about the "g-spot" or the erogenous zone, but I do know that in this era, those are important places on and in the body that need stimuli in the excitement of giving and receiving sexual pleasure. Certainly, your husband may have presented the ideas to you in an abrasive manner; therefore, it may be more profitable for your marriage if the two of you talk frankly about your inhibitions and his desire to have you (re)light his fire in the comfort of your "garden of Eden" (see Chapter Two) after both of you have taken a moment at the Love Altar (see Chapter One).

Again, be thankful that your husband has presented you with gifts that will enhance your sexual attractiveness and sensuality for him only. He hasn't asked you to parade yourself before his peers—as King Ahasuerus (Xerxes) did to Vashti at the beginning of the Book of Esther. Her husband, the King, demanded her appearance to dance before him and his drunken peers. He wanted to show off his beautiful Queen to his drunken buddies. The King became angry when Vashti refused to be exploited; his buddies were disappointed and angry and encouraged the King to get rid of her, divorce her and get another queen.

Vashti was cast out of the palace (divorced) because

she refused to be humiliated before a crowd of men. She refused to be "eye-candy" for a brood of possibly brutal and violent men. Vashti demonstrated her strength and lack of fear of her husband's authority. The portrayal of King Ahasuerus' behavior in the Esther Scripture is repugnant to the sensibility of any woman who epitomizes dignity and respect for herself and her husband, especially in public.

But consider this, your husband didn't ask you to perform for his buddies. What he asked was that you "put on a show" for him in the privacy of your bedroom. I reiterate the fact that your husband was inebriated when he approached you with these "enhancements" which also repulsed you. Therefore, I strongly suggest that the two of you address the matter of his drinking personally and professionally if the issue is that far-reaching. Both of you should be able to enjoy the fruit of the vineyard in a naturally euphoric state, not just going through the motions with fear, anger and or a "clouded" mind. Please remember, the "drinking" discussion should take place in another designated space (not in the "garden").

Finally, my sister, words exchanged in the heat of an argument can definitely cause hurt feelings. The thing about words is this: Once they're out, you can't get them back. But what you can do is ask for forgiveness and be forgiving. After the two of you have forgiven each other, then turn the page and start anew.

On the new page of your marriage, maybe the two of you

will be able to communicate better and discuss whatever -- whenever necessary. Read books such as "The Five Love Languages" and "The Guide to Great Sex." Look through a catalog to select fantasy lingerie or have the sex toy discussion in earnest if that will enhance your passionate moments together.

You don't have to put your Christianity outside of your bedroom door in order to enjoy sex. Hebrews 13:4 reminds us that marriage is honorable, and the bed is undefiled (free from stain or blemish; not having its purity or excellence debased). Go on, girl! You are liberated through Christ Jesus to love your man with all that is within you.

Resource List

Bedroom Secrets encourages women to seek answers by going before God first in prayer, asking the Holy Spirit for wisdom and revelation. Search the scriptures and see how God enlightens your heart. In addition, women can turn to trusted church leaders or Christian counselors for answers to these and other difficult questions. Books, CDs and DVDs address many of these issues. And progressive ministers, leaders and teachers are beginning to talk about sex in the church as well as during conferences and other events.

Please check out these suggested resources that will assist you in "Enhancing Your Garden of Eden."

Books

Red Hot Monogamy
Bill and Pam Farrel
Did you know the best sexual experiences are enjoyed by married couples? Bill and Pam Farrel use insight, humor, and candid personal perspectives to help couples ignite passion in marriage.

Pure Pleasure: Making Your Marriage a Great Affair
Bill and Pam Farrel (co-authored with Jim and Sally Conway)
To order: Go to www.farrelcommunications.com.

Creating an Intimate Marriage --DVD curriculum Kit
Jim Burns
Shows couples how to make marriage a priority as they repair the past, resolve conflict, refresh their marriages spiritually, and more.

Intimate and Unashamed: God's Design for Sexual Fulfillment
Scott Farhart
Addresses a wide range of topics for young and single, newlyweds, or long-time married couples. A safe resource with accurate medical information based on godly principles.

To order both of these resources: Go to Homeword.com and click on ShopHomeword

Ministers and Counselors

Pam Farrel is the author of more than 25 books, including best selling Men are like Waffles, Women are like Spaghetti, 10 Best Decisions a Woman Can Make, Woman of Influence, 10 Best Decisions a Parent Can Make, Fantastic After 40, Devotions for Women on the Go!, Red Hot Monogamy, and Got Teens? She is the co-director of Farrel Communications and Masterful Living. She is also the founder of Seasoned Sisters. For more information, go to www.farrelcommunications.com, www.seasonedsisters.com, or call 800-810-4449.

Minister Linda Moody, founder of Healing for Our Nations, speaks to teens, singles, and married couples about the importance of pursuing holiness and faithfulness in marriage or and singleness and thereby preventing the spread of sexually transmitted diseases. Her workshop for couples, "So You Thought the Grass Was Greener," encourages couples to be faithful within their marriages and makes them aware of the dangers of infidelity due to STDs.

Willie Hubbard and his wife Nell lead national and international workshops on communication, sex and money. Hubbard is pastor of the District Heights Church of Christ in Maryland. For information, call (301) 568-1071.

Rev. Dr. Susan Newman is the author of Oh, God: A Black Woman's Guide to Sex and Sexuality. In addition to providing marriage counseling, she encourages couples and individuals to find sex therapists for counseling through the American Association of Sexuality Educators, Counselors and Therapists at www.aasect.org.

The National Institute of Marriage
Hollister, MO
(417) 335-5882

New Life Ministries
This nonprofit responds to the needs of those seeking healing and restoration through God's truth.
(800) NEW LIFE

Notes

Notes

Chapter Five
Stay In the Right Frame of Mind

The Power of the Lie

Satan is called "the ruler of this world" (John 12:31) therefore he indirectly influences our thoughts/mind through the world around us. The Hebrew word for "Satan" means "enemy." The Greek word for "devil" means "slanderer." Satan's most frequent and consistent attack is directed against our minds. He comes with an arsenal of weapons: lies, threats and intimidation, questions, accusations, lust and other enticements. The only thing he really has left is the LIE. Prepare yourself for spiritual warfare associated with the LIE.

Dear Bedroom Secrets:
About a year ago, I met a man online. I was going to this chat room for people who like to collect African American memorabilia and artifacts. I started talking to this guy named "Gerald" who's a new collector. He collects old films and books on the African American experience. Anyway, we started talking more and more frequently in the chat room. Then we started talking outside the chat room, just the two of us.
It didn't seem to be a problem at first. He said he's married. I'm married. My husband isn't as "adventurous" in the bedroom as he used to be, if you get my meaning. He's slowed down a bit, and he works hard. Yes, I am grateful for him, and we've raised a good family. Our youngest will be graduating from high school soon. But my husband doesn't share my interests. He doesn't make my pulse race anymore. This guy does. I can't wait to talk to him online. I think about him all day. I wonder what he's doing, what he looks like. We seem to have such a connection.
My husband and I -- we can only connect over the kids, and the house, you know? He didn't go to college. I have a degree in fine arts, and Gerald is so intelligent. We have such deep conversations. We talk about everything. I've told him some of my deepest fears and secrets -- things and desires about which my husband has no clue.
The older my husband gets, the more boring he seems. And he's never supported my dreams, not really. He thought going back to school for my degree was silly because at the time, our kids were still kind of young. I still get angry when I think about how I still had to work, cook, clean and then study late at night with almost no help

from him. He paid the bill and that was it. I no longer can remember what I saw in my husband.

Well, here's the thing: Gerald wants us to meet in person. He says it's time to meet so we can see if we really have something special. He lives near the beach in Florida. I can see it now -- long walks by the ocean, moonlit nights, and endless conversation—connecting in person, heart-to-heart.

My husband would think I was at a collectors' conference. He doesn't like to go to these events. The last time we went to a conference, he stood around looking like an idiot. The other collectors and I were examining slave memorabilia and talking about how far the black race had come now that Barack Obama was the Democratic nominee for the U.S. presidential election. My husband just stood back with his hands in his pockets. I was so embarrassed to be there with him. I'd rather go alone.

So what should I do? I feel like a 15-year-old girl experiencing her first crush! I don't want to hurt anybody, but I don't want to lose my last chance at happiness. What about me?

Dear SisterGirl,

What about you? The first thing I'd say is this: "You've made a gargantuan mistake. STAY AWAY FROM THE CHAT ROOM!" Then, I'd want you to identify your real purpose for visiting the chat room in the beginning—was it for African American memorabilia and artifacts or were you shopping for companionship? After all, I also see in your letter that you're having some concerns about your marital relationship, or least about the man to which you are married.

A few things I want you to think about: (1) Does one need to have a college education in order to appreciate African American memorabilia and artifacts? (2) Do you talk about your husband, and does "Gerald" talk about his spouse during these Internet/phone conversations? (3) From your husband's perspective: do you still make his 'pulse race'? (4) How can you share your deepest fears and secrets with a stranger—and your husband don't have a clue about them? (5) Are you becoming fearful of being left with your husband when the last child has gone off to college? (6) Do you know from where this resentment comes? (7) Are you willing to do the "work" on behalf of your husband/family (compare Proverbs 31:10-31)? (8) Are you willing to lose the trust of your husband should this "new" thing not work out? (9) Do you really know your husband?

You'll win or lose the battle for your marriage in your mind. If you harbor resentment, bitterness, unforgiveness or anger toward your mate, your heart will grow hard and others will appear far more tempting. Likewise, such an attitude could push your spouse away from the marriage.

While you're reflecting on the questions I asked earlier, reflect on these five things to help you Stay in the Right Frame of Mind::

- **Keep an atmosphere of respect in your marriage:**

When negativity consumes you, I suggest you take it to the Love Altar (see Chapter One). Confess your heart to your Heavenly Father. When you pour out your heart in this safe place, love will overtake negativity and give you a different perspective. Further, meditate on scriptures such as the following:
Get rid of all bitterness, rage and anger, brawling and slander, along with every form of malice. Be kind and compassionate to one another, forgiving each other, just as in Christ God forgave you Ephesians 4:31-32 (NIV).

Do not repay anyone evil for evil. Be careful to do what is right in the eyes of everybody. If it is possible, as far as it depends on you, live at peace with everyone. Do not take revenge, my friends, but leave room for God's wrath, for it is written: "It is mine to avenge; I will repay," says the Lord. On the contrary, "If your enemy is hungry, feed him; if he is thirsty, give him something to drink. In doing this, you will heap burning coals on his head." Do not be overcome by evil but overcome evil with good Romans 12: 17-21 (NIV).

- **Renew your mind daily by staying in the Word:**

Search God's Word to find other Scriptures that deal with your heart attitude. Be humble enough to allow God to deal with you first. Be the change you want to see in your marriage.

- **Maintain an attitude of gratitude and appreciation:**

God's Word says, "Whatsoever things are true,

whatsoever things are honest, whatsoever things are just, whatsoever things are pure, whatsoever things are lovely, whatsoever things are of good report ...think on these things" (See Philippians 4:8). Fill your mind with the right kind of thinking about your spouse and marriage

- **Go back to the Love Altar on a daily basis to begin the cycle of love anew with your spouse.**

If you and your husband don't have similar interests, that's fine! Find other satisfying things in which you two can mutually participate.

- **Remember your spouse is a gift!**

Today, more than ever, we all need to know how to Speak Life into our marriages. Your marriage doesn't have to bear the scars of infidelity, pain, ruin or separation. Purpose today that you will begin Speaking Life into your husband so that you can keep the passion and sexual spark alive in your marriage.

Notes

About the Author

Deborah Leaner is a dynamic, energizing, motivational speaker, preacher, and spiritual life coach. She is the founder and chief executive officer of Deborah Leaner Ministries (DLM). The mission of DLM is to equip, restore, and transform women through the word of God. In 2003, Mrs. Leaner also founded Divine Discipleship for Sisters, a discipleship ministry for women.

In 2004, she co-authored a four-book series entitled "New in Him Every Day," designed to help individuals develop a deeper level of intimacy with Christ by "Knowing Who You Are in Christ," "The Power of Prayer," "Spiritual Warfare," and "One-on-One Evangelism Through Journaling." After five years of serving women from various churches in the Washington, DC, metro area, Divine Discipleship for Sisters will continue to serve women ministry leaders through churches nationwide by training women ministry leaders or the pastor's designee to disciple their women.

Mrs. Leaner is married to Deacon Tony Leaner. Together they serve in ministry at their church, First Baptist Church of Glenarden, under the pastoral leadership of John K. Jenkins, Sr.

The Leaners founded the Korey "Alex" Leaner Foundation after the loss of their son in 2005. The foundation provides one-on-one and group mentoring and life-skills training for at-risk youth.

For more information please visit us on the web:

www.DeborahLeaner.com

Notes

Notes

Notes